Big Animal Trainer

ODD JOBS

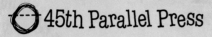

45th Parallel Press

Published in the United States of America by Cherry Lake Publishing
Ann Arbor, Michigan
www.cherrylakepublishing.com

Content Adviser: Eric Weld, Film and Television Animal Trainer, Los Angeles, CA
Reading Adviser: Marla Conn MS, Ed., Literacy specialist, Read-Ability, Inc.

Photo Credits: © Stephen Coburn/Shutterstock, cover, 1; © Paisan Changhirun/Shutterstock, 5; © Wollertz/Shutterstock, 6; © Photos 12 / Alamy Stock Photo, 9; © helenecanada/istock, 11; ©Anan Kaewkhammul/Shutterstock, 13; © phloxii/Shutterstock, 14; © Jens Wolf/dpa/picture-alliance/Newscom, 17; © P.Preeda/Shutterstock, 19; © Hulton-Deutsch Collection/ CORBIS, 21; © Rhbabiak13/Dreamstime.com, 23; © Nejron Photo/Shutterstock, 25; ©oleksa/Shutterstock, 26; © Blueice69caddy I Dreamstime.com - Shamu Killer Whale Photo, 29; © ARENA Creative/Shutterstock, cover, multiple interior pages; © oculo/Shutterstock, multiple interior pages; © Denniro/Shutterstock.com, cover, multiple interior pages; © PhotoHouse/Shutterstock, multiple interior pages; © Miloje/Shutterstock, multiple interior pages

45th Parallel Press is an imprint of Cherry Lake Publishing.

Library of Congress Cataloging-in-Publication Data

Names: Loh-Hagan, Virginia.
Title: Big animal trainer / by Virginia Loh-Hagan.
Description: Ann Arbor : Cherry Lake Publishing, 2016. I Includes index.
Identifiers: LCCN 2015049851I ISBN 9781634710930 (hardcover) I
    ISBN 9781634711920 (pdf) I ISBN 9781634712910 (pbk.) I
    ISBN 9781634713900 (ebook)
Subjects: LCSH: Animal training—Juvenile literature.
Classification: LCC GV1829 .L64 2016 I DDC 791.3/2—dc23
LC record available at https://lccn.loc.gov/2015049851

Cherry Lake Publishing would like to acknowledge the work of The Partnership for 21st Century Skills.
Please visit *www.p21*.org for more information.

Printed in the United States of America
Corporate Graphics Inc.

Contents

Champions to Big Animals

Who are some famous big animal trainers? What do they do?

Everyone loves a circus. Big cats jump through burning hoops. Elephants balance on their back legs. Bears ride bikes.

Big animal trainers work with these animals. They teach them to do tricks. Patricia White is known as the "beauty with the beasts."

She teaches big cats to perform for circuses. She controls the 500-pound (227 kilograms) beasts. She said, "I've had a few minor accidents and some close calls, but nothing serious. I know my animals."

She was attacked by a young cat. It lasted five seconds. She escaped. She hurt her back. She had a tiger tooth stuck in her arm. She had cuts on her stomach. Her nose was ripped. She healed. She was angry at herself. She learned to pay more attention.

A popular animal circus trick is putting body parts in the mouths of dangerous animals.

Tim Sullivan manages a zoo near Chicago. He's in charge of animal training.

Sullivan trains his animals to work for a living. He wants the animals to find their own food. He wants animals to see **habitats**, not zookeepers, as their food source. Habitats are places where animals live. He wants to make zoo life similar to wild life. This makes animals more active.

Zoo animal trainers want zoo habitats to look natural.

DR. VAIDYANATHAN KRISHNAMURTHY

Dr. V. Krishnamurthy was an Indian animal doctor and elephant trainer. He was known as "Dr. K" or the "Elephant Doctor." He improved the ways people capture and train elephants. He said, "I love elephants and they love me." He worked with many elephants. He worked with them for over 50 years. He was never attacked. He was famous for helping to capture an elephant that killed 15 people in India. Dr. K had a special relationship with an elephant named Inspector General. They were friends for over 20 years. Inspector General had been in a fight with wild elephants. Dr. K. healed Inspector General's wounds. When Inspector General died, Dr. K. visited his grave. People say great elephant trainers aren't made, they're born.

He worked with gorillas. His team created a special box with treats. Gorillas figured out how to get food out. He changed the behavior of zoo gorillas. Animal training is about growing an animal's abilities.

Randy Miller trains big animals to be stars. His company is called Predators in Action. He stages animal attacks for movies, television, and commercials. He's worked with tigers, lions, cougars, leopards, and bears. He lives with his animals. He has a mountain home.

Years ago, a cougar attacked some bikers. This happened in California. One biker was killed. Another biker was cut up. Miller trained his cougars to re-create this scene. This was for a television show. The show is called *Fight to Survive.*

Miller also trains actors. He trained Chris Pratt for his role in *Jurassic World.*

Miller shows actors how to react to animals when filming.
Even if the animals aren't real!

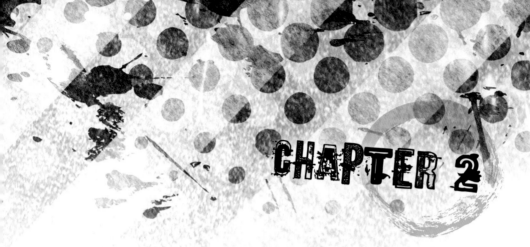

CHAPTER 2

Getting Big Animals to Listen

What makes big animal trainers special? How do they train big animals?

Most trainers train dogs, horses, or seals. Big animal trainers are special. They train big animals. Big animals include tigers, elephants, and orcas. Big animals are usually wild animals.

Trainers work for zoos, circuses, theme parks, or the movie business. They train animals for working or performing.

Mahouts are Indian elephant trainers. They train elephants to be ridden, to perform in religious events, and to work.

Zoos train animals for practical reasons. Big animals have to be fed, cleaned, and studied. Zoo trainers teach animals to stand, lift limbs, and lay down. They train them to behave for zookeepers, doctors, and researchers.

Other big animal trainers teach animals to perform. They focus on tricks.

Big animal trainers teach animals to respond to **commands**. Commands are orders. They want animals to behave in a certain way.

They reward good behavior. Food is a common reward. Trainers practice a lot. They repeat behaviors. They want animals to develop habits.

Good trainers don't hurt animals. They use tools to communicate. They use **guides**. Guides are sticks. The guides may have food on them. Animals follow the guides.

Some trainers use whips, hooks, and prods in harsh ways. But most trainers would never hurt their animals. They know trainers should build trust. They should make animals feel safe.

Trainers at zoos and theme parks have stable work locations. They also have regular hours. Circus and movie

Big animal trainers get animals to respond to auditory, physical, and visual cues.

trainers work all hours of the day. They travel a lot. They train animals to travel.

Trainers also **groom** the animals. They wash them. They cut their nails. They feed them. They clean their homes. They exercise them. They monitor their health.

Big animal trainers also train actors and performers. They teach them to interact with animals. They teach humans to respond better to animals. Trainers teach wild animals to adapt to humans.

Caring for animals is a 24-hour-a-day, 7-day-a-week job.

Big Animal Trainer
KNOW THE LINGO

Approximations: small steps toward the behavioral goal

Arena: the large cage in which big cat acts are performed

Big cat presenter: circus trainer of performing lions and tigers

Big five: lions, leopards, rhinos, elephants, and African buffalos

Boss elephant man: the person in charge of the circus elephants

Breaking: the first stages of animal training

Bull tub: heavy, round metal pedestal upon which an elephant sits or stands

Chuff: a sound tigers make similar to quickly blowing puffs of air out of their mouths

Flehman: behavior when big cats inhale with their mouths, then open and curl their upper lips to smell better

Handler: another word for trainer

Jackpot: a big reward for a big effort

Menagerie: a collection of animals that may be shown or exhibited

Ring stock: animals that perform in a circus show

Shaping: building a behavior in gradual steps

Temperament: aspects of animals' personalities that they're born with

Training to be a Trainer

What do people need to do to become a big animal trainer? What should big animal trainers learn?

Big animal trainers learn on the job. There are different levels. First, there are **apprentice** trainers. They learn from an experienced trainer. Second, there are associate trainers. These are new trainers. Third, there are senior trainers. These are trainers with a lot of experience.

Trainers need a high school degree. They may need special courses. They learn biology, zoology, and animal psychology. They may also take speech or drama classes. They may need to speak in front of large crowds.

Some trainers work with ocean animals. They work with orcas. They need a college degree. They need to be good swimmers. They need to be good divers.

Some big animal trainers learned from family members.

Tamara Reynolds is a big animal trainer. She's worked with tigers in Taiwan. She's worked with wolves in New Zealand. She understands that animals have special personalities. Some are easy to train. Some aren't.

Advice From the Field
ALEXANDER LACEY

Alexander Lacey trains big cats. He's owned his own zoos. He's worked for popular circuses. His advice: Keep out of the line of fire when the animals pee. He learned this from his father. His father was a big animal trainer. They had trained lions. One of the lions peed on a guest. Lacey and his father couldn't stop laughing. Lacey said, "The lion started peeing for three or four minutes." The guest was soaking wet. Lacey has never forgotten that moment. He thinks it's important to know his animals. His job requires him to understand their every move. He said, "We get to know the animals so well that it's difficult for an outsider to understand how you can judge every single movement."

Trainers know a lot about animals. They study animals. They know their needs. They know their habits. They pay attention to their animals.

They love animals. They treat their animals well. They're kind. They're sensitive. They're patient. It may take a long time for animals to learn.

Trainers need to be in shape. They lift heavy objects. They handle the big animals.

Big animal trainers bond with their animals.

CHAPTER 4

From Skinner to Stage

Who helped develop big animal training? Who are famous big animal trainers from the past?

Animals have helped humans for centuries. They've built cities. They've entertained. They've worked. Humans trained animals.

In the 1930s, B. F. Skinner made training into a science. He developed a system. It uses rewards. Treats are given for desired behaviors.

Marian and Keller Breland applied Skinner's research. They started a business. It was called Animal

Behavior Enterprises. They created ways to train animals. They focused on rewards. They trained over 15,000 animals. They worked with over 140 different animals.

Marian Breland and Bob Bailey developed **clicker** training. A clicker is a tool that makes sounds. Trainers click when animals do something correctly. They also give animals a treat.

The Brelands' first job was training farm animals for ads.

WHEN ODD IS TOO ODD!

Training big animals is an odd job. Training tiny animals is even odder. Steven R. Kutcher trains insects. He's known as "The Bug Man of Hollywood." He turns bugs into movie stars. He's worked on over 100 movies. He's also worked on television shows, music videos, commercials, and online ads. He manipulates insect behaviors. He changes how they respond to light, air pressure, and gravity. He gets bugs to perform tricks. He trained a wasp to fly into an actor's mouth. He trained a cockroach to run across the floor and flip on its back. He trained a spider to crawl into a shoe. He trained a scorpion to power up a cell phone. He trained bees to swarm on camera. He trained a fly to walk through ink and leave footprints. This led to his "bug art." He used insects as "living brushes."

Clyde Beatty was a circus **showman**. He was a performer. His famous act combined polar bears and big cats. In the 1920s, he was known as "America's youngest and most fearless wild animal trainer." He developed the image of a lion tamer. He walked into cages with big cats. He pretended to be scared. He carried a whip and a chair. He acted like the boss.

Gunther Gebel-Williams was inspired by Beatty. He trained lions to ride on horses. He trained elephants to walk through busy traffic. He performed over 12,000 shows.

He was different than Beatty. He didn't want to be boss. He respected the animals. He said, "I worked with tigers as a trainer, never a tamer."

The circus played a major role in big animal training.

CHAPTER 5

Big Dangers!

What are the dangers of being a big animal trainer? What are some issues of big animal training?

Working with big animals is risky. Big animals are big. They're heavy. They have sharp teeth. They have sharp claws. They're wild. They're **unpredictable**. Their behaviors are uncertain.

Tyke was a circus elephant. He ran through a crowd. He killed one circus worker. He hurt another worker. He was shot to death.

Circus elephants have run away from circuses. They've run through streets. They've crashed into buildings. They've attacked people.

Big animal trainers risk their lives. Big animals could push trainers. They could press them against walls. They could kick them. They could hurt them. They could kill them.

Trainers must learn to calm their animals.

Stephan L. Miller was Randy Miller's cousin. He was a big animal trainer. He was making a video. He worked with a bear. The bear's name is Rocky. Rocky is almost 8 feet (2.4 meters) tall. He weighs 700 pounds (317 kg). He's a bear actor. He's trained to wrestle humans.

Stephan Miller and Rocky stood next to each other. Rocky stood in his wrestling position.

Big animal trainers need to be safe and smart.

THAT HAPPENED?!?

Carl Hagenbeck was a German animal trainer and dealer. He collected and sold animals. He helped design the modern zoo. His son, Heinrich, took over the business. He wanted to combine different animals in the same space. Edmund Heller agreed. Heller was a zookeeper. He worked in Milwaukee's Washington Park Zoo. He combined three grizzly bears, three polar bears, five black bears, and three wolves. It didn't work. Two polar bears drowned a black bear in a pool. The black bear died. The other animals ate its body. Heller tried again. A year later, a polar bear drowned another black bear. A month later, the same thing happened. Heller finally separated the animals.

Some big animal trainers believe they are educating people about animals.

Something happened. He jumped early. Miller was surprised. He couldn't raise his arm. He couldn't defend himself. Rocky bit Miller's neck. Miller quickly died.

Some people wanted to kill Rocky. They thought he was dangerous. Others thought it wasn't right for wild animals to be trained. Miller's death was accidental. So, Rocky was allowed to live.

Dawn Brancheau worked at a theme park. She trained orcas. Orcas weigh 12,300 pounds (5,579 kg). She was performing a show. The orca attacked her. It yanked her by her ponytail. It dragged her to the pool bottom. She died.

This upset many people. They were sad about Brancheau's death. They also worried about the animals. They think wild animals should stay in the wild. They think humans mistreat animals.

Big animal training is not for everyone. It's hard. It's scary. It's **controversial**. This means not everyone agrees with it. But trainers find it rewarding. They love their animals.

DID YOU KNOW?

- Male lions are 100 times harder to train than tigers. Lions are also better fighters. Dave Hoover was a big animal trainer. He worked for Cole Brothers Circus. He said lions had killed some of his circus tigers.

- Elephants are the world's largest land animals. They have the largest brains. They're very smart. They have emotions. They're easy to train. Younger elephants are easier to train than older elephants. Asian elephants are easier to train than African elephants.

- The American Humane Association protects animals. It monitors the use of animals in movies. It makes sure animals are safe. But it doesn't monitor animal training.

- A horse was killed while making a movie. It was an accident. This happened in 1939. The PATSY Award was created. PATSY stands for Picture Animal Top Star of the Year. It honors animal performers. Francis the Talking Mule received the first award.

- Bettina Browne trained tigers for *We Bought a Zoo*. She thinks house cats are harder to train. House cats work with her only "if they feel like it."

- It's not easy to train a giraffe. It takes three trainers to trim a giraffe's nails. One trainer climbs a ladder and feeds the giraffe. The second trainer holds the ladder. Meanwhile, the third trainer trims the hoof.

- Mahouts have been taming elephants for over 5,000 years. They are given elephants as young boys. They bond to their elephants for life.

CONSIDER THIS!

TAKE A POSITION! Some people think circuses shouldn't have animals. They believe in animal-free circuses. This would mean big animal trainers could lose their jobs. Do you agree or disagree with animal-free circuses? Argue your point with reasons and evidence.

SAY WHAT? Learn more about dog training. Explain the differences and similarities between training dogs and big animals. (Explain the differences between domesticated and wild animals.)

THINK ABOUT IT! Tigers naturally fear fire. But they're trained to jump through fire hoops. Tigers are active at night. But they're trained to perform in daytime. Female elephants do not naturally stand. But they're trained to stand on their back legs. Should humans be training wild animals to do unnatural tricks?

SEE A DIFFERENT SIDE! Some people think training big animals is cruel treatment. They believe big animals should live in the wild. Learn more about their position. Why do they think big animal training is inhumane?

LEARN MORE: RESOURCES

PRIMARY SOURCE

Sutherland, Amy. *Kicked, Bitten, and Scratched: Life and Lessons at the World's Premier School for Exotic Animal Trainers*. New York: Viking, 2006.

SECONDARY SOURCES

Helfer, Ralph, and Ted Lewin (illustrator). *The World's Greatest Elephant*. New York: Philomel Books, 2006.
Spiotta-Dimare, Loren. *Performing Horses: Horses That Entertain*. Berkeley Heights, NJ: Enslow Publishers, 2014.

WEB SITES

American Society for the Prevention of Cruelty to Animals: www.aspca.org
Big Cat Rescue: http://bigcatrescue.org

GLOSSARY

apprentice (uh-PREN-tis) a person learning from someone more experienced

clicker (KLIK-ur) a device that makes noises

commands (kuh-MANDZ) orders, directions

controversial (kahn-truh-VUR-shuhl) debatable, sparking disagreements

groom (GROOM) to clean

guides (GIDE-urz) sticks that lead animals

habitats (HAB-ih-tats) places where animals live

showman (SHOH-mun) a performer

unpredictable (uhn-prih-DIK-tuh-buhl) not able to be predicted or determined

INDEX

ABOUT THE AUTHOR

Dr. Virginia Loh-Hagan is an author, university professor, former classroom teacher, and curriculum designer. As soon as you meet her dogs, you'll realize she doesn't know anything about training animals. She lives in San Diego with her very tall husband and very, very naughty dogs. To learn more about her, visit www.virginialoh.com.